A true story from the Bible

JOSEPH and the very STRANGE DREAMS

WRITTEN BY
Tim Thornborough

ILLUSTRATED BY
Jennifer Davison

There are lots of lovely words in the world. And many words have opposites.

The opposite of in is out. The opposite of left is right. The opposite of happy is sad.

In this true story from the Bible, we're going to follow the story of Joseph, his brothers and his dad. It's a story with lots of ups and downs — keep an ear out for all the opposites.

So join me as we follow the bad-good, near-far, sleep-awake, worried-calm story of what happened when Joseph started to have some Very Strange Dreams.

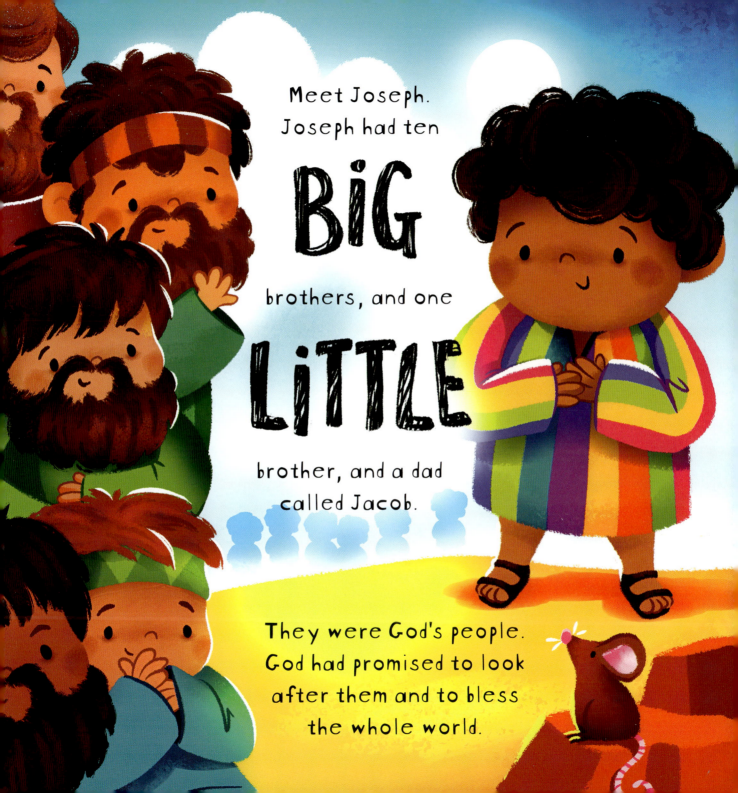

Meet Joseph. Joseph had ten BIG brothers, and one LITTLE brother, and a dad called Jacob.

They were God's people. God had promised to look after them and to bless the whole world.

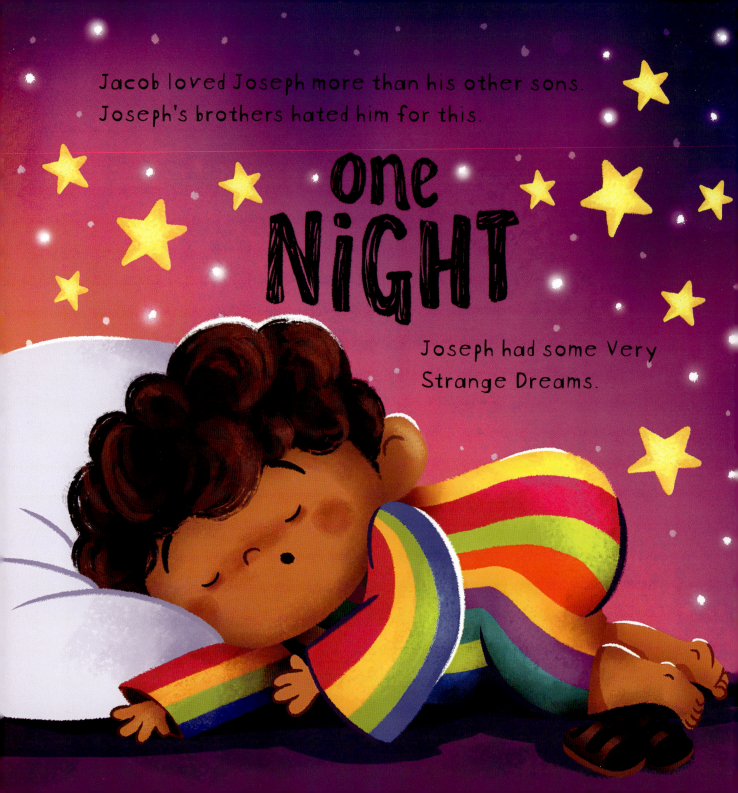

Jacob loved Joseph more than his other sons. Joseph's brothers hated him for this.

One Night

Joseph had some Very Strange Dreams.

The next DAY he told his family about them.

"We were gathering bundles of wheat. Your bundles all bowed down to my bundle."

"Then the sun, moon and stars all bowed down to me."

Joseph's brothers did not like the idea of bowing down to him.

They were so angry that they threw him **DOWN** a well to die.

Joseph had been FREE but now he was a SLAVE. Then he ended up in prison.

His life had been **GOOD** but now it had gone very **BAD.**

But Joseph remembered God's promises. He knew that...

The Lord has a plan, and he's working it out.

He speaks words we can trust, so there's no need to doubt.

God told Joseph what they meant.

And just three days later they all came true.

The butler was set free and went to work for Pharaoh – the King of Egypt.

One night in the PALACE

Pharaoh had a Very Strange Dream. He did not know what it meant. The butler told Pharaoh all about Joseph, who could explain dreams.

Joseph was brought to see the king.

"The Lord has told me what your Very Strange Dreams mean," he said.

"There will be seven years when **LOTS OF FOOD GROWS,**

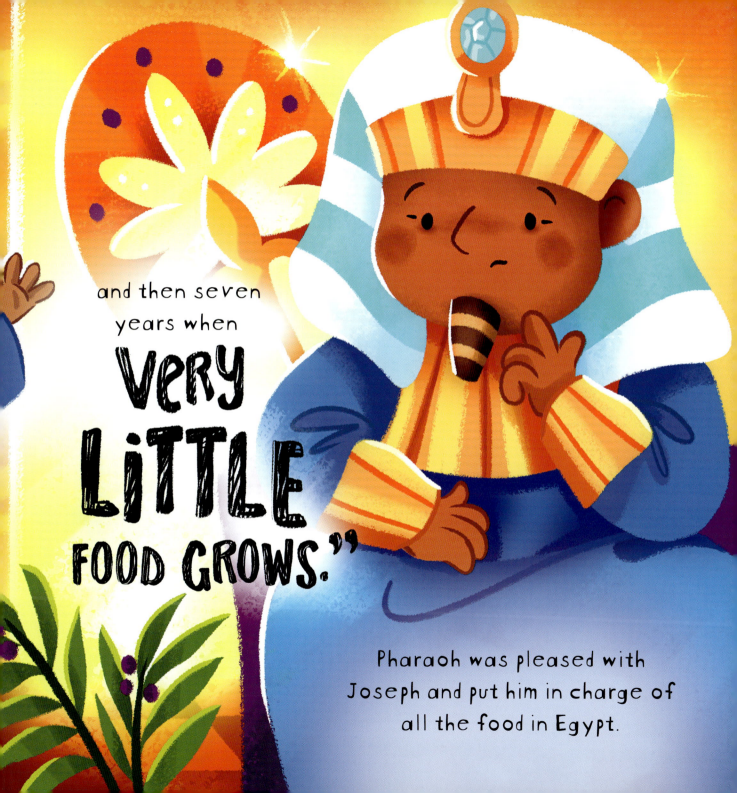

and then seven years when **VERY LITTLE FOOD GROWS."**

Pharaoh was pleased with Joseph and put him in charge of all the food in Egypt.

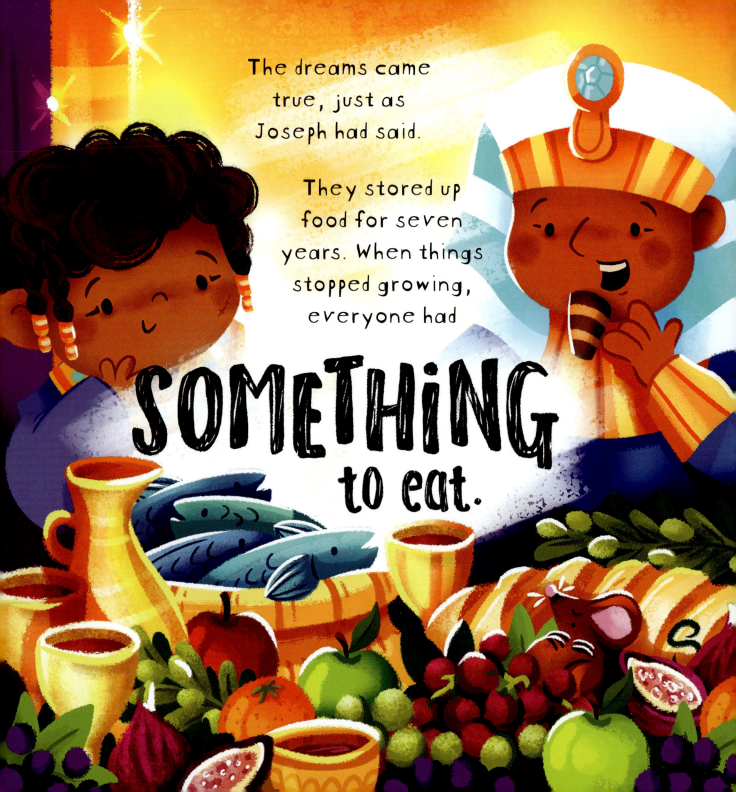

The dreams came true, just as Joseph had said.

They stored up food for seven years. When things stopped growing, everyone had SOMETHING to eat.

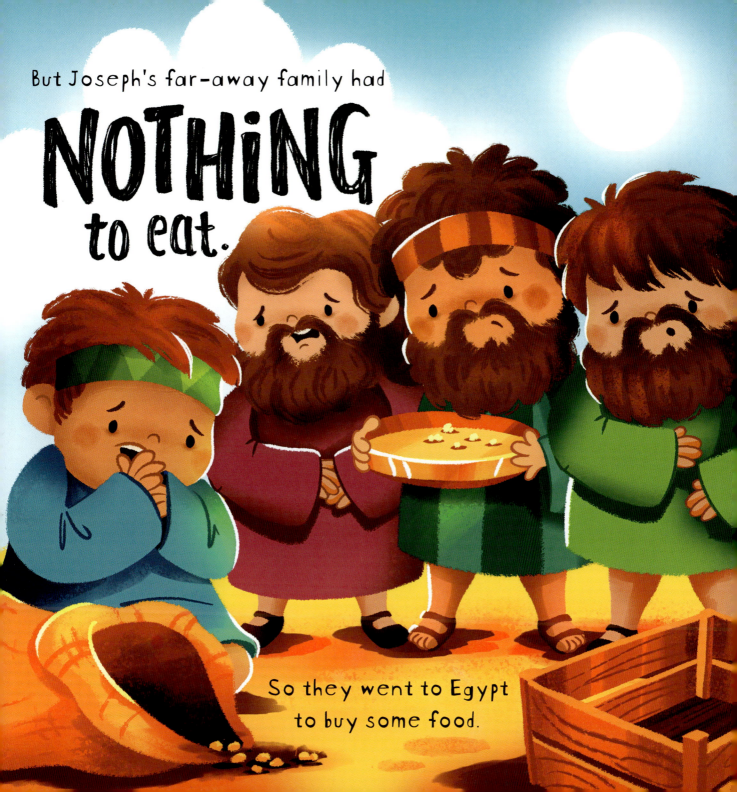

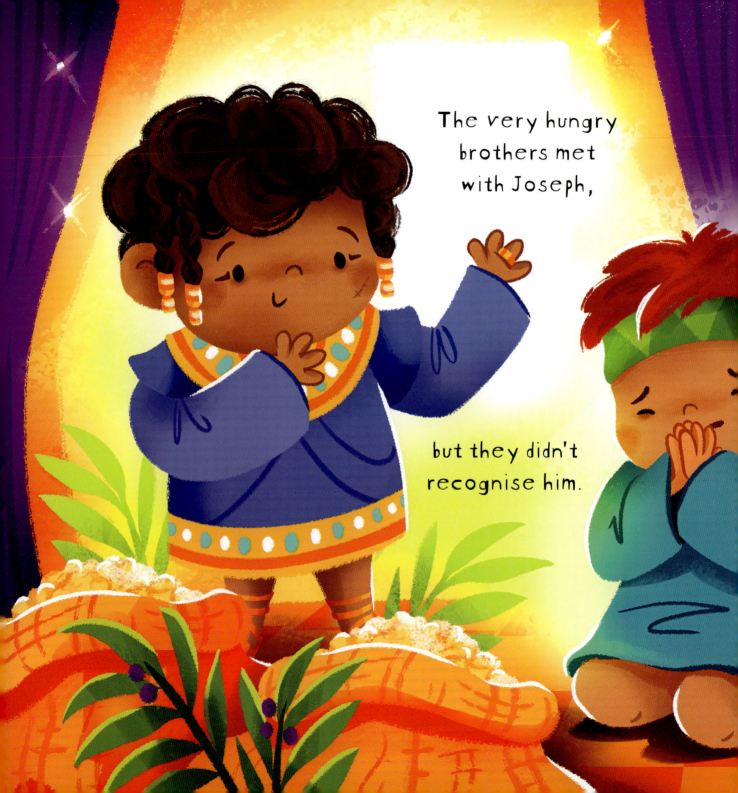

They bowed down low to him – just like in his Very Strange Dreams about wheat and stars all those years before.

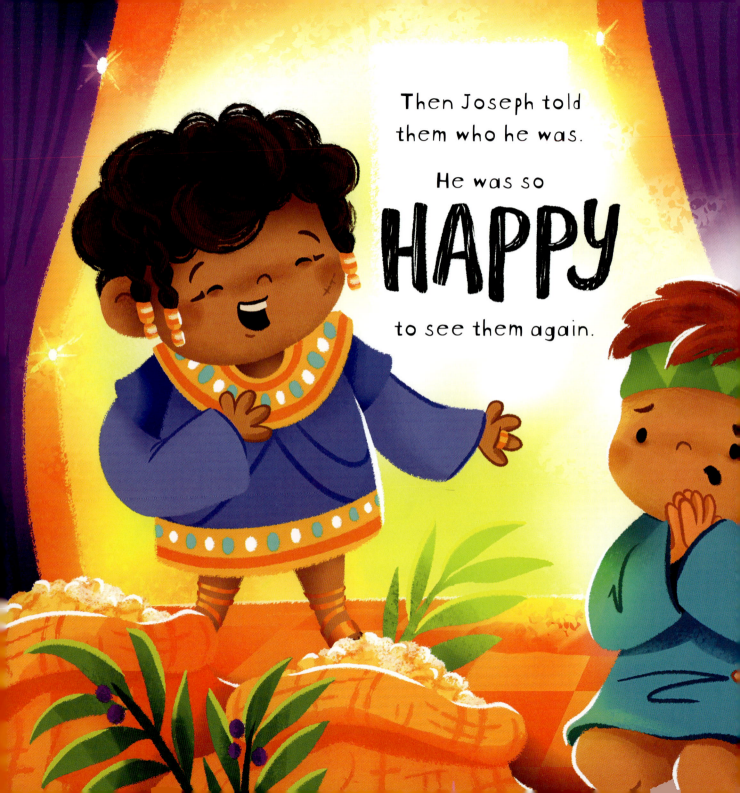

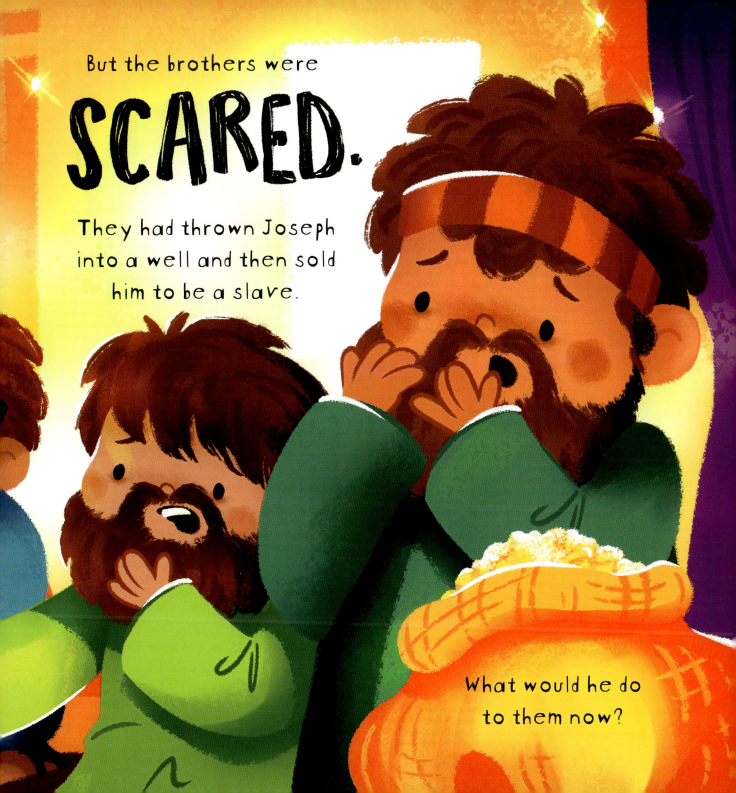

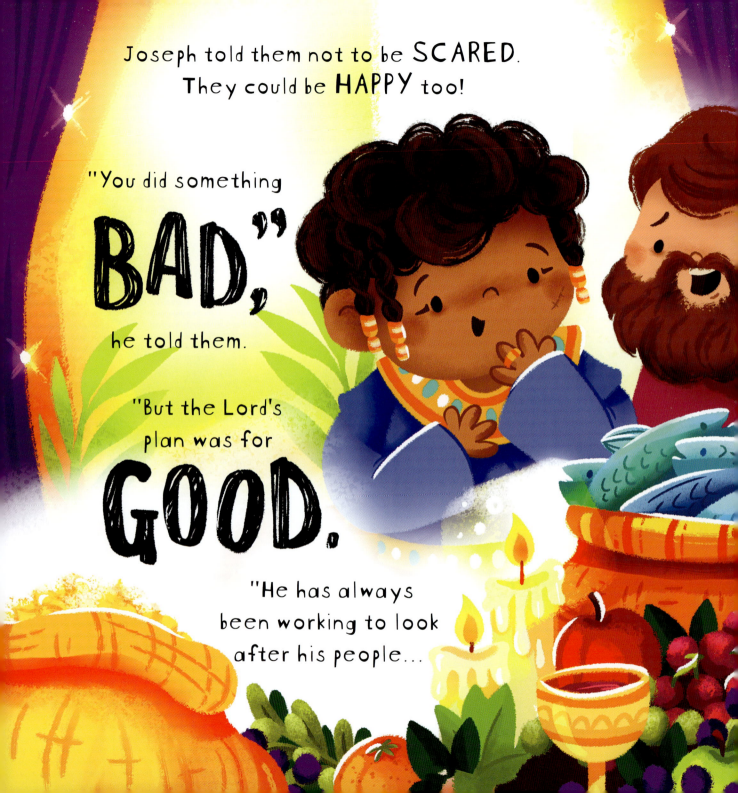

Joseph told them not to be SCARED. They could be HAPPY too!

"You did something **BAD**," he told them.

"But the Lord's plan was for **GOOD**.

"He has always been working to look after his people..."

"even when you did very wrong things and even when I had to face very hard things."

God has a plan to look after his people and bless the whole world.

We can remember what Joseph remembered:

Enjoy all of the Very Best Bible Stories Series:

 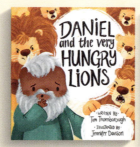 
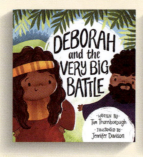 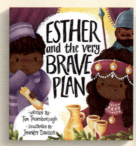 
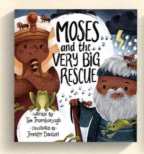 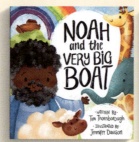 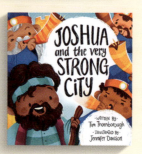

thegoodbook.com/vbbs | .co.uk/vbbs